Opossums

PHOTOS AND FACTS FOR EVERYONE

BY ISIS GAILLARD

Learn With Facts Series

Book 111

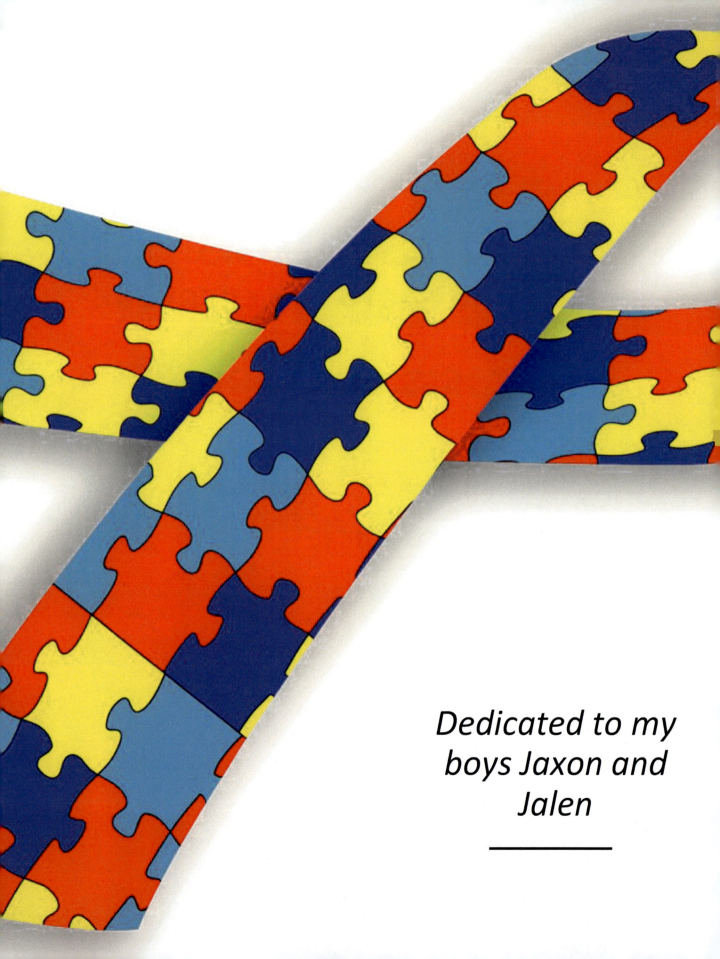

Dedicated to my boys Jaxon and Jalen
_____

CONTENTS

Isis Gaillard. Opossums: Photos and Facts for Everyone (Learn With Facts Series Book 111). Ebook Edition. Learn With Facts an imprint of TLM Media LLC

eISBN: 978-1-63497-234-5
ISBN-13: 978-1-63497-364-9

Introduction

Opossums originated in South America and crossed the Atlantic Ocean in the Great American Interchange once the continents were linked. Their unspecialized biology, adaptable nutrition, and reproductive habits enable them to colonize and survive in a variety of environments.

In North America, there are several dozen different species of opossum, which are commonly referred to as possums. The Virginia opossum, often known as the common opossum, is the only marsupial (pouched mammal) found in both the United States and Canada.

Opossums are easily recognizable by their long tails, pointed faces, and huge, hairless ears. They are the only marsupial species in North America. Their coats are typically gray in hue. However, they can range from red to brown. The pests' thick fur also has long, white-tipped guard hairs, giving them a grizzled appearance. Opossum tails are hairless and serve as an extra leg for climbing.

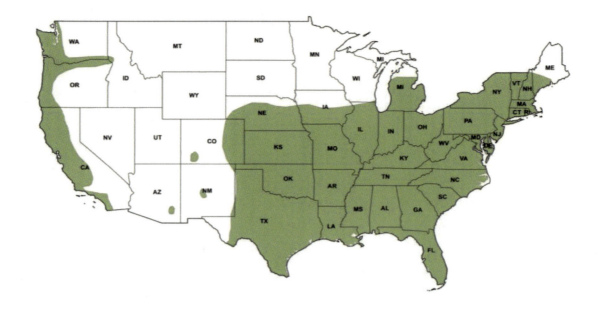

The common opossum and Virginia opossum are found in the United States, Mexico, Central America, South America and Canada. Though they aren't picky about where they hang out, opossums love trees and will stay aloft in trees as much as possible. They also prefer areas that are wet, like marshes, swamps and streams.

Possums sleep in nests in hollow trees or dens inside caves, attics, and abandoned buildings on the ground. They don't like the light, so they usually find places that are well covered during the day to sleep. Typically, any place well-covered, safe from predators, and free will be perfect for a possum to sleep in.

Description

The average opossum is about the size of a housecat. The nose of these marsupials is extended, and they have a big sagittal crest — a bone that makes their forehead appear taller. They have scaly feet and a prehensile tail with scaly scales.

The average opossum is about the size of a housecat. The nose of these marsupials is extended, and they have a big sagittal crest — a bone that makes their forehead appear taller. They have scaly feet and a prehensile tail with scaly scales. To keep the animal stable while climbing, a prehensile tail can be wrapped around the branches.

These opossums have a pink tip to their cone-shaped nose, a long hairless tail, and white, gray, and black fur. The only marsupial found naturally in North America is the opossum.

Opossums can reach a length of 40 inches, which is about the same as a house cat. They have white or grayish hair covering their body. Opossums have a rat-like tail and a long, pointed face with round, hairless ears. The opossum is primarily dark gray in color, but some resemble cinnamon, and, as in Heidi's case, white opossums are known to exist. The possum is primarily gray in color. The possum and the opossum are both hunted animals and possess an instinct to play dead or "play possum" when threatened.

Size

Length: Virginia opossum: 35 – 94 cm, Common opossum: 30 cm
Mass: Virginia opossum: 0.8 – 6.4 kg, Common opossum: 1.2 kg
Opossums are about the size of small dogs.

They are about 2.5 feet (76 centimeters), nose to tail, and weigh 8.8 to 13.2 lbs. (4 to 6 kilograms), according to National Geographic

Breeding

The Virginia opossum's breeding season can start as early as December and last until October, with most babies born between February and June. Each year, a female opossum may have 1-3 litters. The male attracts the female during mating season by generating clicking sounds with his mouth.

At Austin, it's opossum breeding season. After a three-month anoestrous interval, Texas begins in January. In the third week, the modal point for ovulation days is reached.

The rate of intra-uterine development was primarily explored by surgically removing one uterus, recording the stage attained by the ova therein, and leaving the remaining uterus to incubate its ova a. a time span that has been pre-calculated Unique graphs exemplify the results. The primitive-streak stage, as well as the medullary groove and chords, have been accomplished. Begin seven and a half days after coitum and seven days after ovulation, leaving only five and a half days for embryo growth before birth. The development rate is compared to that of Eutherian mammals.

The curvature of the postnatal development curve is similar to that of higher animals' embryonic growth curve. At around fifty days, the eyes and mouth open. The young leave the tent for the first time at this point, but they are not weaned for another thirty days. The mother may become pregnant again soon after weaning. The young may begin to shift for itself at ninety to one hundred days (young size of giant rats).

As they battle to reach their mother's fur-lined pouch, where only 13 mammary glands usually await them, up to half of them perish within minutes. The babies grow quickly, doubling in size every 7 to 10 days.

Based on animals gin-trapped in 800 ha of indigenous forest in the Orongorongo Valley, near Wellington, the growth of pouch young and juvenile Trichosurus vulpecula to maturity is described. Opossums were captured consistently for a year, starting in March 1953 and then irregularly until 1961.

Eating Habit

Dead animals, insects, rodents, and birds are all eaten by opossums. They eat eggs, frogs, plants, fruits, and grain. Opossums devour the skeletal remains of rodents and roadkill animals to meet their calcium requirements. Opossums also eat dog, cat, and human food waste.

Many large opossums (Didelphini) are immune to the poison of rattlesnakes and pit vipers (Crotalinae) and often hunt on them. This adaptation appears to be unique to the Didelphini, as their closest relative, the brown four-eyed opossum, is not resistant to snake venom.

Eating Habit

It's been proposed that Didelphis opossums and crotaline vipers are engaged in an evolutionary arms race. Some researchers believe this adaptation evolved as a defense mechanism, allowing for a rare reversal of an evolutionary arms race in which the former prey has become the predator, while others believe it evolved as a predatory adaptation because it also occurs in other predatory mammals and does not occur in opossums that do not regularly eat other vertebrates.

Interesting Facts

1. Opossums and Rabies - While an opossum can carry the rabies virus, it is exceedingly unlikely. Opossums have a strong immune system and a low body temperature. Because of these characteristics, the opossum is less likely to contract rabies.

2. Playin' Possum - Did you happen to come upon a "dead" opossum in your yard? Perhaps you came upon one curled up by the side of the road? Don't even think about picking up the shovel! Opossums are amazing at seeming to be dead, to the point of being picked up and carried away. Many opossums have been killed by well-intentioned humans who mistakenly bury a "dead" opossum in their yard or run over a "dead" opossum on the side of the road.

3. Nature's Garbage Men - Opossums eat carrion, which is dead animals, in the same way as vultures do. Decomposing carcasses can readily spread some fairly nasty diseases, especially those that can make people sick. Scavengers inhibit disease spread by eating dead animals. Scavengers have advanced immune systems, so they can eat the carrion without contracting illnesses that would otherwise be fatal.

THE END

Thanks for reading facts about Opossums. I am a parent of two boys on the autism spectrum. I am always advocating for Autism Spectrum Disorders which part of the proceeds of this book goes to many Non-Profit Autism Organizations. I would love if you would leave a review.

Author Note from Isis Gaillard:

Thanks For Reading! I hope you enjoyed the fact book about Opossums.
Please check out all the Learn With Facts and the Kids Learn With Pictures series available.

Visit www.IsisGaillard.com and www.LearnWithFacts.com to find more books in the Learn With Facts Series

More Books In The Series

Over 75 books in the Learn With Facts Series.

Set 1

```
A  L  L  X  R  F  K  Y  S  A  S  I  X  K  P
S  Q  H  Y  N  O  W  O  G  R  B  G  S  O  W
E  L  X  D  B  X  O  B  A  I  A  D  O  R  R
L  G  W  B  Z  E  U  Y  T  L  R  G  F  R  D
E  K  G  O  O  S  B  X  Z  I  A  V  U  U  F
P  L  D  W  H  I  E  H  B  E  I  S  Y  O  S
H  S  D  V  I  C  E  C  T  E  Y  W  C  H  C
A  C  H  I  N  C  H  I  L  L  A  S  A  I  J
N  S  S  B  N  N  F  A  F  J  L  T  Y  A  L
T  O  E  U  T  O  F  P  M  V  E  D  C  I  S
S  O  D  S  M  F  S  V  T  E  R  S  O  W  R
E  R  Z  O  R  A  G  A  H  Y  L  N  Q  V  A
A  A  F  E  L  O  T  C  U  I  S  E  Q  Y  E
G  G  Q  R  G  P  H  O  K  R  A  K  O  L  B
L  N  T  C  X  X  H  Z  P  F  S  E  A  N  B
E  A  L  I  S  E  L  I  D  O  C  O  R  C  S
S  K  D  E  K  V  W  S  N  D  P  N  D  Z  I
S  G  O  H  E  G  D  E  H  S  O  P  F  G  I
F  H  S  R  E  V  A  E  B  P  C  C  I  B  S
A  H  B  P  E  G  I  R  A  F  F  E  S  H  E
```

Word List

Bears
Beavers
Birds
Chameleons
Cheetahs
Chinchillas
Cougars
Crocodiles
Dinosaurs

Dolphins
Eagles
Elephants
Foxes
Frogs
Giraffes
Hedgehogs
Hippopotamus
Horses

Kangaroos
Koalas
Lions
Owls

Set 2

```
Z  G  K  M  V  B  E  E  S  S  O  V  E  E  P
P  E  A  C  O  C  K  S  F  R  A  N  E  Y  H
G  I  P  Z  A  L  L  I  G  A  T  O  R  S  B
C  J  G  A  E  N  F  V  S  U  U  L  Y  C  R
Y  R  R  U  N  L  X  Z  R  G  Q  K  C  S  C
H  S  I  F  A  D  L  Y  E  A  N  O  E  I  K
R  P  C  D  H  N  A  E  G  J  T  I  P  H  S
H  I  F  A  N  W  A  S  I  X  P  O  X  N  S
I  D  Z  A  M  A  P  S  T  P  Q  I  E  A  Y
N  E  F  L  H  E  S  B  U  X  T  T  R  G  H
O  R  L  P  G  M  L  P  T  O  T  B  B  S  S
C  S  A  A  U  M  D  S  A  I  E  A  L  E  I
E  A  M  C  E  N  W  S  K  Z  T  C  R  A  F
R  A  I  A  A  U  N  D  M  S  R  T  W  T  Y
O  L  N  S  S  I  N  K  S  E  F  F  V  U  L
S  J  G  Z  U  A  V  E  N  R  R  T  K  R  L
G  O  O  G  S  O  C  B  A  H  S  I  A  T  E
D  I  N  T  F  C  B  Y  K  Q  Z  C  B  L  J
B  E  A  Q  B  U  T  T  E  R  F  L  I  E  S
P  C  I  N  S  E  C  T  S  E  V  Q  K  S  Z
```

Word List

Alligators	Flamingo	Penguins
Alpacas	Gazelle	Rhinoceros
Bats	Hyena	Sea Turtles
Bees	Iguanas	Snakes
Butterflies	Insects	Spiders
Camels	Jaguars	Tigers
Cats and Kittens	Jellyfish	Zebras
Dogs and Puppies	Pandas	
Fish	Peacocks	

Set 3

```
P  S  G  U  K  P  O  N  I  E  S  C  M  M  S
O  A  N  S  O  C  T  O  P  U  S  E  S  I  E
T  T  R  O  E  R  O  O  S  T  E  R  S  Q  A
C  S  K  R  I  F  K  K  J  M  Y  P  W  S  L
M  Y  J  A  O  P  O  V  J  L  C  I  A  G  S
W  K  C  Q  E  T  R  W  E  S  U  G  N  G  A
H  Z  E  F  I  Y  S  O  R  A  V  S  S  O  N
W  O  L  V  E  S  P  A  C  E  S  A  S  S  D
L  G  Y  Z  W  A  E  S  S  Y  N  W  T  S
V  X  T  L  R  B  D  O  N  D  O  D  N  R  E
H  G  I  D  R  R  O  A  Y  G  S  P  S  I  A
W  E  S  A  A  M  C  G  A  T  T  I  E  C  L
U  H  L  Z  X  I  G  R  P  A  A  G  A  H  I
L  O  I  E  L  T  D  E  K  B  R  L  H  E  O
P  L  O  E  X  O  U  R  I  S  F  E  O  S  N
L  N  P  Q  D  A  E  R  D  G  I  T  R  N  S
B  R  P  O  V  E  S  W  T  X  S  S  S  V  S
A  E  M  L  M  L  Y  N  X  L  H  T  E  W  G
D  O  O  X  X  O  W  H  A  L  E  S  S  H  M
K  V  R  A  N  T  E  A  T  E  R  S  A  J  T
```

Word List

Anteater	Parrots	Starfish
Komodo Dragons	Pelicans	Swans
Leopards	Pigs and Piglets	Turtles
Lizards	Polar Bears	Whales
Lynx	Ponies	Wolves
Meerkat	Roosters	
Moose	Scorpions	
Octopuses	Seahorses	
Ostriches	Seals and Sea Lions	

Set 4

```
Z P O R C U P I N E S C M F Z
P K N S K C E O Y U H A O A I
E C H I D N A R F M O E U A H
K H C K W Q E E S E R R N K F
R M P L S E U K Y G O A T S X
N A R L D Q R J N E C H A P V
S H C N A O U U G B H P I B L
T Y I C T T P I U B I L N B I
C E E S O F Y F R E C T L Z V
R O G K E O F P Z R K D I S E
F D W I N A N L U R E O O L D
E W I S L O G S L S N L N O N
R E T O V V D X U A S G S T A
R C H I P M U N K S M W W H I
E W S H A R K S D Q S A M S N
T I D Y C Z O O T H O R A D A
S Y T E G U I N E A P I G S M
J S E T E S E E R D L O J T S
J K H H F R P S K U N K S N A
X A R M A D I L L O C E R L T
```

Word List

Armadillo
Buffalo
Chickens
Chipmunks
Cows
Deer
Donkeys
Echidna
Emu

Ferrets
Goats
Guinea Pigs
Llama
Mountain Lions
Platypus
Porcupines
Raccoons
Reindeer

Sharks
Sheep
Skunks
Sloths
Squirrels
Storks
Tasmanian Devil

Set 5

```
3  W  M  S  E  S  I  O  T  R  O  T  T  X  M
0  Q  M  A  R  S  U  P  I  A  L  S  S  S  V
D  B  G  Z  R  J  A  D  D  G  V  B  C  E  A
A  A  V  V  H  I  S  L  A  M  M  A  M  T  N
N  S  L  A  M  I  N  A  M  R  A  F  S  O  T
G  B  J  B  K  X  S  E  Y  O  X  R  M  Y  E
E  G  A  E  T  U  X  K  L  P  X  I  U  O  L
R  P  U  M  R  N  C  F  S  I  C  C  S  C  O
O  C  U  L  O  A  O  L  R  B  F  T  S  F  P
U  M  A  F  T  J  E  U  S  V  R  E  O  Y  E
S  W  V  T  F  S  I  R  B  A  E  I  P  A  S
A  C  L  M  A  I  U  U  M  D  P  J  O  A  A
N  E  X  E  I  M  N  P  A  N  T  H  E  R  S
I  M  W  G  E  M  H  S  I  T  I  H  B  D  G
M  X  T  L  P  I  Y  F  B  U  L  T  N  V  R
A  J  A  D  B  G  A  S  Q  R  E  B  C  A  L
L  T  D  I  Y  B  K  N  R  K  S  Q  W  R  B
S  P  A  P  V  O  S  O  J  E  S  W  F  K  D
U  N  V  B  N  O  D  L  G  Y  S  J  V  S  Y
S  J  G  O  R  I  L  L  A  S  A  S  A  E  H
```

Word List

30 Dangerous Animals
Aardvarks
Amphibians
Antelopes
Cattle
Coyotes
Farm Animals
Gorillas
Lemurs

Mammals
Marine Life
Marsupials
Opossums
Panthers
Puffins
Reptiles
Tortoises
Turkeys

Walrus
Weasels
Yaks

Set 1

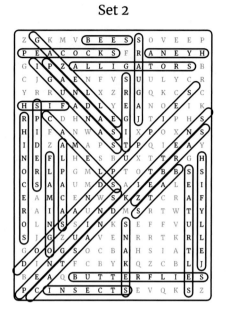

Set 2

Set 3

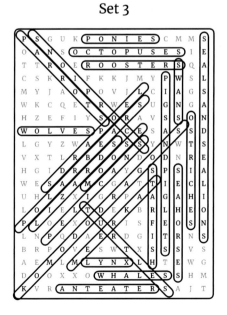

Set 4

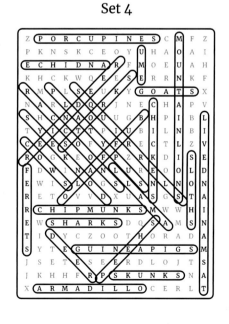

Set 5

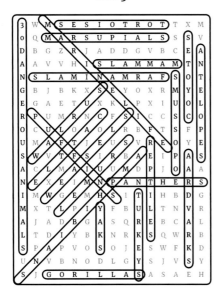

Puzzle 1

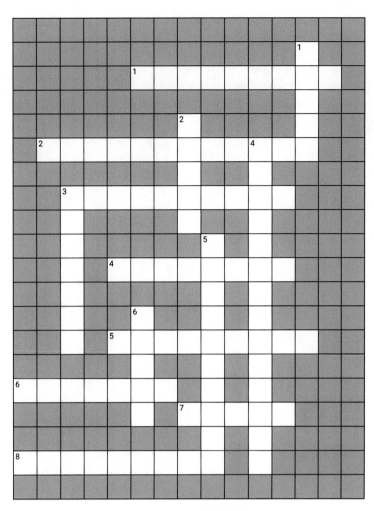

ACROSS
1. Dinosaurs
2. Caterpillars
3. Crocodiles
4. Dolphins
5. Hedgehogs
6. Beavers
7. Foxes
8. Elephants

DOWN
1. Frogs
2. Birds
3. Cougars
4. Apes and Monkeys
5. Chameleons
6. Bears

Puzzle 2

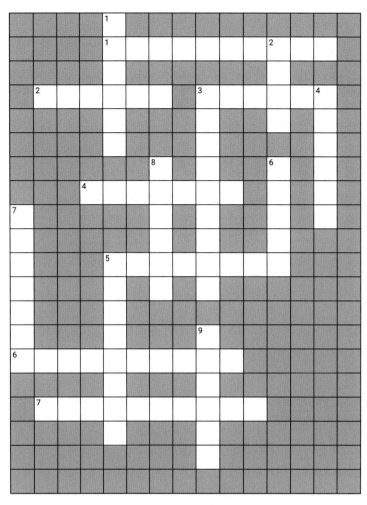

ACROSS
1. Alligators
2. Tigers
3. Koalas
4. Alpacas
5. Peacocks
6. Sea Turtles
7. Rhinoceros

DOWN
1. Camels
2. Owls
3. Kangaroos
4. Snakes
5. Penguins
6. Lions
7. Spiders
8. Pandas
9. Zebras

Puzzle 3

ACROSS
1. Meerkat
2. Lizards
3. Fish
4. Parrots
5. Hyena
6. Leopards
7. Iguanas
8. Gazelle
9. Insects

DOWN
1. Jellyfish
2. Jaguars
3. Ostriches
4. Octopuses
5. Bats
6. Flamingo
7. Moose
8. Lynx

Puzzle 4

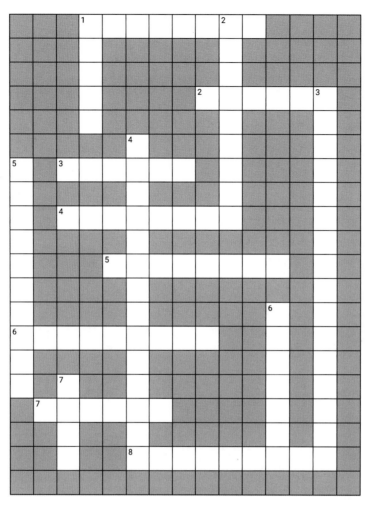

ACROSS
1. Starfish
2. Whales
3. Ponies
4. Roosters
5. Anteater
6. Armadillo
7. Wolves
8. Scorpions

DOWN
1. Swans
2. Seahorses
3. Seals and Sea Lions
4. Pigs and Piglets
5. Polar Bears
6. Buffalo
7. Cows

Puzzle 5

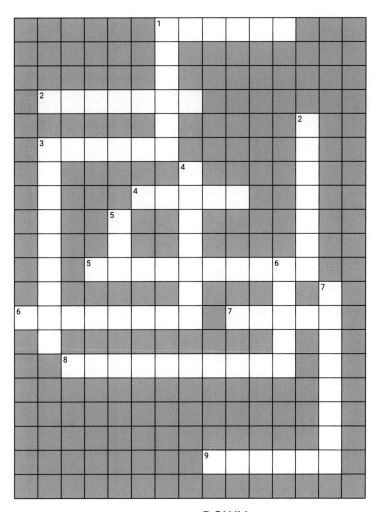

ACROSS
1. Sloths
2. Echidna
3. Storks
4. Sheep
5. Guinea Pigs
6. Platypus
7. Llama
8. Porcupines
9. Sharks

DOWN
1. Skunks
2. Donkeys
3. Squirrels
4. Ferrets
5. Emu
6. Goats
7. Raccoons

Puzzle 6

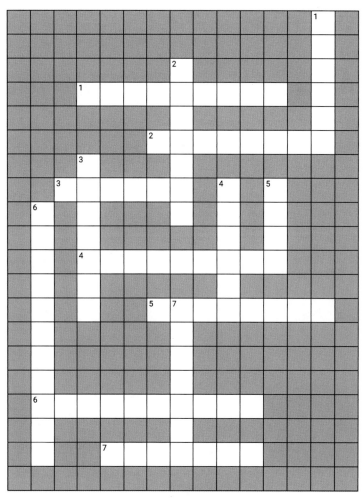

ACROSS
1. Tortoises
2. Gorillas
3. Cattle
4. Aardvarks
5. Opossums
6. Amphibians
7. Weasels

DOWN
1. Lemurs
2. Coyotes
3. Mammals
4. Walrus
5. Yaks
6. Farm Animals
7. Puffins

Puzzle 1

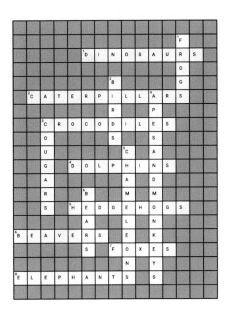

Puzzle 2

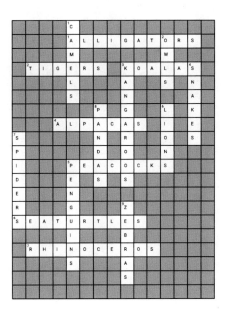

Puzzle 3

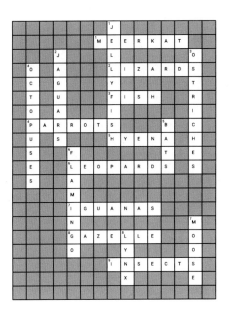

Puzzle 4

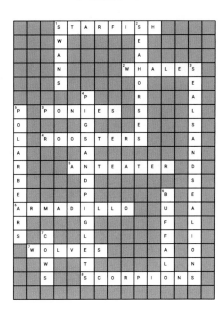

Puzzle 5

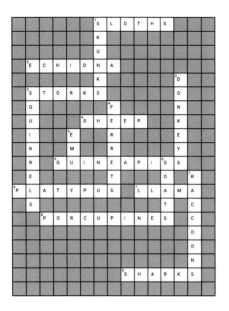

Puzzle 6

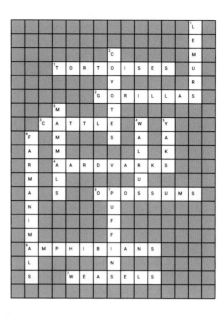

Made in the USA
Las Vegas, NV
17 December 2023